I0457910

MY STORY
OF
HEAVEN

WHAT I SAW AND EXPERIENCED

Harrison Sharma Mungal, Ph.D., PsyD.

Foreword by Pastor Francis Armstrong

My Story Of Heaven

Unless otherwise identified, Scripture quotations are from
New King James Version of the Bible.

Contact author via email:
info@agetoage.ca
www.agetoage.ca
www.harrisonmungal.com
Facebook: Harrison Mungal
Twitter: AgeToAgeInc1
LinkedIn: Harrison Mungal, Ph.D., PsyD
YouTube: Harrison Mungal
Phone: 905-533-1334

ABOUT *the*
AUTHOR

Harrison Sharma Mungal, BTh, MCC, MSW, PhD, PsyD

Dr. Mungal is a devoted therapist with a background in mental health and clinical psychology, driven by a genuine passion for life and the well-being of those under his care. With an impressive literary portfolio comprising over 40 books and a seasoned public speaking career that has reached audiences in over 42 nations, he brings a wealth of knowledge and skills to his practice.

Alongside his professional accomplishments, Dr. Mungal places a high value on family, with a successful marriage of over 35 years, seven children, and multiple grandchildren. In addition to his clinical practice, Dr. Mungal and his wife have played pivotal roles in church planting, pastoral ministry, and missionary work, even during the challenging times of the Cold War in Croatia from 1994-1997. They have nurtured congregations, established churches, and served as missionaries, demonstrating a deep commitment to spreading the gospel. Their dedication extended to running a Bible college, Metro Bible College, for over a decade before transitioning into mental health and addictions counselling.

Dr. Mungal is widely respected for his unique ability to blend biblical principles with scientific insights, adding a distinctive "psychology twist" to his therapeutic approach. He explained God made us Body, Soul (mind, will and emotions) and Spirit. As much as people need support physically and spiritually, "the soul is where people are wounded and is in need of healing." His expertise has been sought after by various media outlets, including appearances on television programs including 700 Clubs Canada and 100 Huntly St. He has also been invited to speak at prestigious institutions such as the Attorney General of Canada, police departments, hospitals, community agencies, and churches. His contributions have earned him accolades and recognition from local authorities, police departments, mayors, community leaders, and countless families.

With over 21 years of experience in mental health, psychiatry, and psychology, coupled with over four decades dedicated to teaching and preaching the gospel, Dr. Mungal possesses a wealth of expertise in both fields. His educational background is equally impressive, with a Christian Leadership Certificate, a Ministerial Diploma from two years of Bible College, a bachelor's degree in Theology, two master's degrees (in Counselling and Social Work), and two doctorate degrees (in Social Work and Clinical Psychology).

In summary, Dr. Mungal's journey is a testament to his unwavering commitment to serving others, integrating his faith with his professional expertise to make a positive impact in the lives of countless individuals, couples, and families. His multifaceted career reflects a deep sense of purpose and a profound dedication to promoting holistic healing and spiritual growth.

Table of Contents

FOREWORD

Having immersed myself in Dr. Harrison Mungal's book, "My Story Of Heaven," and pondered the profound image he saw in our church, I can't shake the conviction that the door to heaven or the heavenly realms is more substantial than any earthly counterpart.

Jesus himself proclaimed that He is the door, the gateway through which we access these celestial realms. As we step through this divine threshold, we encounter a stairway, a pathway adorned with angels ascending and descending. Jesus serves as both the door and the stairway into these realms where heavenly messengers traverse.

My prayer for all who engage with this book is that they come to a deeper understanding of the reality of heaven. It's not merely a distant concept but a tangible realm where miracles, signs, and wonders abound.

Moreover, Jesus promised that what we experience in this heavenly realm can manifest here on earth, aligning our earthly existence with the glory and authority of God's kingdom. This realm isn't reserved solely for the afterlife; it's accessible to each of us here and now. It's a realm overflowing with the presence of God and the power of His kingdom.

As you journey through the revelations shared in this book about heaven, may you be profoundly blessed and enlightened. God bless you abundantly as you embark on this journey.

Warm regards,
Pastor Francis Armstrong

INTRODUCTION

Stepping into the realm of sharing my encounter with God's throne room has been a journey sparked by a single moment—an unexpected convergence of past and present. It all began during a speaking engagement at Third Day Worship with Pastor Francis Armstrong, where I was met with a surprise that would reignite memories long dormant within me.

As I made my way into the sanctuary, I couldn't ignore the photo displayed prominently on the social media screens—the very image that graces the cover of this book. In an instant, it transported me back over four decades to the profound encounter I had with God's presence, a moment that has left an indelible mark on my soul.

It's been over 40 years since I first experienced the awe-inspiring majesty of God's throne room, yet the memory remains as vivid as ever. The surge of power, the warmth, and the palpable presence that enveloped me upon entering that sacred space—it all came rushing back with startling clarity.

Standing before the imposing doors, I felt the reassuring presence of the Holy Spirit by my side, guiding me through this divine encounter. And as those doors swung open, revealing the breathtaking beauty beyond, I was overcome with a sense of wonder and awe that words cannot fully capture.

In the pages of this book, I offer but a glimpse into the magnificence of God's throne room—a place where the glory of God shines brightly, and His presence fills every corner.

Through my journey, you'll discover insights into creating an atmosphere conducive to encountering God, the profound significance of worship, and a vivid description of the throne room itself.

This book is more than just a recounting of my personal experience—it's an invitation to embark on a transformative journey of your own. As you delve into the pages that follow, may you be inspired, uplifted, and forever changed by the boundless love and glory of God. Welcome to " My Story Of Heaven."

AN *open* ENTRANCE

You know, thinking about heaven always gives me a sense of wonder and curiosity. It's like this beautiful mystery waiting to be explored, with its open entrance inviting us to discover its wonders. The Old Testament paints vivid pictures of what heaven might be like, offering glimpses of its glory and splendor. It's fascinating to imagine what awaits us beyond this earthly realm, beyond the struggles and trials we face in our daily lives.

As I delve into the scriptures, I'm struck by the way the Old Testament lays the groundwork for our understanding of heaven. It's like finding clues to a hidden treasure, each passage revealing a little more about the beauty and majesty that awaits us. From the visions of prophets to the descriptions of heavenly realms, the Old Testament paints a rich tapestry of what heaven might be like.

But more than just a distant dream or a far-off destination, heaven holds a special place in our hearts as believers. It's a place of hope and promise, a place where we long to be reunited with our loved ones and experience the fullness of God's presence. And while the Old Testament gives us glimpses of heaven, it's through the life, death, and resurrection of Jesus Christ that we truly understand its significance.

Entering into the heavenly realm is not reserved for a select few; it's an open invitation for anyone who desires to encounter the presence of the Lord. Let me paint a picture for you, one that illuminates just how accessible it truly is to enter into the glorious presence of God.

Picture a spiritual tabernacle, meticulously crafted according to the divine blueprint revealed to Solomon, Moses, and David. This sacred design serves as our pathway into the heavenly realms, where the glory of the Lord awaits. Just like the ancient tabernacle, there are steps and stations we must navigate to reach the Holy of Holies—the inner sanctum where the presence of God dwells in its fullest measure.

Unfortunately, many people falter and lose heart before they ever taste the sweetness of heaven's embrace. They grow weary along the journey, never fully experiencing the tangible presence of God that awaits them. But I'm here to tell you that it doesn't have to be this way. With the right guidance and understanding, every believer can access the heavenly realms and encounter the glory of the Lord in profound ways.

In the days of the Old Covenant, this privilege was reserved solely for the high priest. But now, in the New Covenant, every believer has been granted this remarkable access. It's a profound honor bestowed upon each of us—a divine invitation to step into the spiritual tabernacle where the glory of God resides. Just as there were three entrances into the Holy of Holies in the ancient tabernacle, we can identify three key waypoints on our journey to encounter God's glory.

Looking at it from another perspective, we can also discern three crucial waypoints that lead us to experience the power of God in our personal lives. These waypoints serve as pivotal moments in our spiritual journey, marking the progression from mere knowledge of God to intimate encounter with His power and presence. As we navigate through these depots, we unlock deeper levels of spiritual insight, intimacy, and empowerment.

First comes the hearing of the message—a pivotal moment that often occurs in the outer court of our spiritual journey. It's where we encounter the truth of the Gospel, sparking a curiosity within us to explore further.

As I reflect on my own journey, I remember the initial stirrings of interest, the questions that arose, and the sense of wonder as I began to grasp the significance of Christ's message.

Next comes the pivotal decision to invite Christ to be the Lord of our lives—an essential step akin to entering the Holy Place. It's where we make a deliberate choice to surrender to His lordship, allowing His presence to permeate every aspect of our being.

I recall the moment when I made this decision, the weight lifted off my shoulders, and the newfound sense of purpose and direction that ensued.

Then comes the profound experience of being filled with the Holy Spirit—a sacred encounter likened to entering the Holy of Holies. It's where we are enveloped in the presence and power of God in a tangible way.

As I think back on this moment in my own journey, I am reminded of the overwhelming sense of peace, joy, and empowerment that flooded my soul as the Holy Spirit took residence within me.

This sacred encounter transforms mere belief into vibrant faith, as the reality of God's presence becomes palpable. It's a turning point where our faith is no longer confined to religious rituals or outward observance but becomes deeply personal and transformative. It's in this place that our commitment to serving God is solidified, as we are propelled by the power of His Spirit to live out our faith authentically and passionately.

Without reaching this place of encounter, we risk remaining as mere shells of Christianity—going through the motions, but lacking the dynamic power and presence of God in our lives. It's a sobering realization that prompts me to continually seek deeper intimacy with God, knowing that true fulfillment and purpose are found in His presence.

In the Old Testament, the intricate details of the tabernacle served as a symbolic representation of the deeper spiritual truths and realities we can experience in our relationship with God.

As I could recall what I saw aligned with the scriptures, I discover the rich symbolism embedded within the construction and layout of the tabernacle, each element pointing to a profound spiritual reality.

One of the key elements of the tabernacle was the entrance, referred to as the Door or gate. As I reflect on the descriptions provided in Exodus 27:16-17 and Exodus 38:18-19, I am struck by the meticulous craftsmanship and symbolism woven into its design.

The hanging for the gate of the court, made of intricately woven materials—blue, purple, scarlet, and fine twined linen—served as a visual reminder of the access we have to God's presence.

The dimensions and materials used in constructing the gate were not merely practical considerations but held profound spiritual significance. The colours represented different aspects of God's character—blue symbolizing His heavenly nature, purple signifying royalty, scarlet representing redemption, and fine twined linen representing purity and righteousness.

As I ponder on these details, I am reminded of the invitation extended to us to enter into God's presence, clothed in His righteousness and cleansed by the blood of Christ.

Furthermore, the pillars and sockets made of brass, with hooks and overlaying of silver, speak of the strength and stability of our access to God. The silver, symbolizing redemption, reminds me of the price paid for our access to God through the sacrifice of Jesus Christ. The four pillars and sockets represent the firm foundation upon which our faith stands, rooted in the finished work of Christ on the cross.

As I contemplate these symbolic representations, I am reminded of the invitation extended to each of us to enter into the presence of God. Just as the gate provided access to the courtyard of the tabernacle, so too are we invited to enter into the presence of God through the finished work of Jesus Christ. It is a reminder of the grace and mercy extended to us, granting us access to the riches of His presence and the blessings of His kingdom.

In my journey of faith, I often reflect on the profound significance of Jesus' words in John 10:1-9, John 14:6, and Acts 4:12. Jesus, in His teachings, referred to Himself as the door or the gate—the entrance through which all must pass. As I meditate on these scriptures, I am reminded of the crucial importance of this initial step in our spiritual journey.

Just as the priests in the Old Testament were required to enter the tabernacle through the gate before performing their duties, so too must each of us embark on our own personal journey of faith.

It is not enough to rely solely on the experiences or testimonies of others; there comes a moment when we must personally encounter the Lord for ourselves. This encounter marks the beginning of a transformative relationship with Christ, where we become born-again believers.

For me, this moment of entering through the gate at 14 years old, represented a pivotal turning point in my life—a moment of decision and surrender to the lordship of Jesus Christ. It was a deeply personal experience, one that cannot be fully understood or appreciated by merely observing from the sidelines. It required active engagement and a willingness to step into the unknown, trusting in the guidance and leading of the Holy Spirit. And once you taste of heaven of this place, you heart and mind crave to be there.

In encountering Jesus as the door, I have discovered a profound sense of belonging and purpose. No longer am I a passive observer of Christianity, but an active participant in the kingdom of God. Through faith in Jesus, I have found forgiveness, redemption, and newness of life. My relationship with Him has become the foundation upon which I build my life, guiding my decisions and shaping my identity.

As I continue to walk through the door that is Jesus Christ, I am continually reminded of His exclusive role as the only way to salvation. Acts 4:12 reinforces this truth, declaring that there is no other name under heaven given among men by which we must be saved. In a world filled with competing ideologies and philosophies, I am anchored in the unwavering truth that Jesus alone is the door to eternal life.

Through the door of Jesus Christ has been a transformative and life-changing experience. It is a journey marked by personal encounter, faith, and surrender—a journey that has led me into the abundant life that Jesus promised. And as I continue to walk through this door, I am filled with gratitude for the grace and mercy extended to me. I am committed to sharing the message of hope and salvation with others who are still searching for entrance.

Through the symbolism of the Tabernacle, I am drawn to the significance of the Brazen Altar. This sacred place served as the site for offering animal sacrifices unto the Lord, a solemn reminder of the atoning work of Christ. Reflecting on passages like Exodus 38:1-7 and Exodus 27:1-8, I am reminded of the profound truth embedded within this symbolic act.

In John chapters 11 and 12, Jesus engages in discussions about death and its profound connection to His mission. In verse 25 of chapter 11, Jesus declares, "I am the resurrection and the life," foreshadowing His ultimate sacrifice on the cross. Similarly, in chapter 12, Jesus foretells His own death and resurrection, likening Himself to a seed that must die in order to bear much fruit (verse 24). These teachings underscore the significance of the Brazen Altar as the second step in our spiritual journey.

As I contemplate the symbolism of the Brazen Altar, I am reminded of the necessity of sacrifice in the life of every believer. Just as Mrs. K. Kuhlman once remarked, "I've died a thousand deaths before I come to the platform," I recognize the profound truth encapsulated in her words.   The Brazen Altar represents a place of surrender, where we learn to die to our fleshly desires and yield our will to God's purposes.

I have experienced the transformative power of sacrifice at the Brazen Altar. It is a place of profound encounter with the grace and mercy of God, where I lay down my own ambitions and desires at the foot of the cross. Here, I am reminded of the sacrificial love of Christ, who willingly laid down His life for the redemption of humanity.

As I continue to journey through the symbolic landscape of the Tabernacle, I am challenged to embrace the call to sacrificial living. The Brazen Altar serves as a reminder that true discipleship requires a willingness to lay down our lives for the sake of the gospel. Just as Jesus laid down His life for us, so too are we called to offer ourselves as living sacrifices, holy and pleasing to God (Romans 12:1). In this sacred act of surrender, we find true freedom and abundant life in Christ.

The symbolism of the Tabernacle drew my attention to the significance of the Laver. This Basin served as a place of purification for the priests, ensuring that they were ceremonially clean before approaching the presence of God. Reflecting on passages like Exodus 30:18-21 and Exodus 38:8, I am struck by the profound truth embedded within this symbolic act.

In John chapter 13, Jesus provides a powerful illustration of cleansing as He washes the disciples' feet and imparts lessons on servanthood. This act of humility underscores the importance of spiritual cleansing in our lives. Similarly, on the Day of Atonement, the Levitical High Priest would undergo a ritual cleansing before offering sacrifices for the sins of the people (Leviticus 16:4). Jesus' teaching on cleansing serves as a prelude to His ultimate sacrifice on the cross, which provides the cleansing we desperately need.

As I meditate on the significance of the Laver, I am reminded of the importance of spiritual purification in my own life. Just as Jesus washed the disciples' feet, He desires to cleanse us from all unrighteousness and make us pure in His sight (1 John 1:9). This cleansing is not merely external but extends to the innermost recesses of our hearts, where the Holy Spirit convicts us of sin and leads us to repentance.

In John 13:10, Jesus emphasizes the importance of spiritual cleansing for our daily walk. The Holy Spirit illuminates areas of our lives that require purification, guiding us away from paths of darkness and leading us into the light of God's truth.

As we surrender to His cleansing work, we prepare ourselves to enter into the presence of God with reverence and awe.

At this juncture in my spiritual journey, I am reminded that God is holy, and He calls us to holiness in every aspect of our lives (1 Peter 1:15-16). The Laver serves as a poignant reminder that we are called to be vessels of honour, purified and sanctified for God's divine purposes. As I allow the Holy Spirit to cleanse me from within, I am prepared to walk in intimacy with God and to experience the fullness of His presence in my life.

As I reflect on the symbolism of the Tabernacle, my attention is drawn to the significance of the Lampstand. This fourth step or station represents a pivotal stage in our spiritual journey—one that many Christians reach but often remain in without progressing further. In Hebrews 9:2, it is referred to as the sanctuary, a place where the candlestick, the table, and the showbread are housed.

The Lampstand serves as a powerful symbol of the Church, as described in Revelation 1:20. However, on a personal level, it speaks to each individual's responsibility to shine their light in the world. It is at this stage that the Holy Spirit illuminates areas in our lives that need cleansing and transformation.

In Revelation 2:5, we are admonished to remember our first love and to repent, lest our candlestick be removed from its place. This underscores the importance of maintaining our spiritual fervour and zeal for the Lord. The Lampstand represents a turning point—a place where the light of God begins to penetrate our hearts and energize us with His power.

Just as a candle is set on a lampstand to illuminate its surroundings, so too are we called to shine the light of Christ in the darkness of the world around us. Luke 8:16 and Luke 11:33 emphasize the importance of not hiding our light but allowing it to shine brightly for all to see.

The Lampstand is also where the oil, symbolizing the Holy Spirit, is poured out. The amount of oil we receive is directly proportional to our level of intimacy with God and our persistence in seeking Him. The deeper our relationship with God, the greater the flow of the Holy Spirit in our lives.

This stage offers us the opportunity to cultivate a deeper partnership with the Holy Spirit—to know Him as our companion, friend, teacher, and comforter. As we press into God and prioritize Him above all else, we open ourselves up to receive more of His Spirit. It is through this intimate relationship with the Holy Spirit that we are empowered to shine brightly for the glory of God, illuminating the world with His love and truth.

As I explore more into the symbolism of the Tabernacle, my focus shifts to the Table of Shewbread—the fifth station on this sacred journey. Here, the shewbread, also known as the bread of the presence, was continuously displayed (Exodus 25:30). The priests would partake of this bread on the seventh day, a ritual that mirrored the sustenance provided by the Lord to His people. Just as the body of Jesus is symbolized as bread in the Lord's Supper, this stage represents a place of spiritual nourishment and revelation.

In Luke 6:4, we see how Jesus entered the house of God and partook of the shewbread, sharing it with those who were with Him. This act underscores the importance of receiving spiritual sustenance directly from the Lord. Similarly, as believers, we are called to feast on the bread of life, which is Christ Himself. This intimate communion with Christ empowers us to share His life-giving sustenance with others.

This divine encounter with the bread of life occurs within the sanctuary or the Holy Place, as described in Hebrews 9:2. It is here that the Spirit opened the Word to me, guiding me into all truth (John 16:12). We cannot fully embrace the Word without first being led by the Holy Spirit. This truth was emphasized by Jesus Himself before His Last Supper, highlighting the importance of this spiritual nourishment.

Just as Christ partook of the shewbread in the house of God, we are invited to come to the Lord's house and partake of the bread of life. When we receive Christ into our lives, we are filled with His presence and equipped to share His abundance with those around us. Too often, Christians rely on others to feed them spiritually, when God is calling each of us to take a step of faith and partake of His provision directly.

In John 6:35, Jesus declares Himself as the bread of life, promising that those who come to Him will never hunger or thirst spiritually. This profound truth is reiterated throughout Scripture, emphasizing the vital importance of partaking of Christ's life-giving presence. As we feast on the living bread that came down from heaven, we are filled with His life and empowered to live abundantly for His glory.

As I reflected on the significance of the Incense Altar standing there with the Holy Spirit, I was reminded of its symbolic importance in our spiritual journey. Just as incense emits a sweet fragrance, God desires us to be a pleasing aroma to Him. This sacred space within the Holy Place marks a pivotal point in my relationship with God—an opportunity to draw nearer to Him and align my hearts with His will.

In Exodus 30:1-10, we are instructed on the preparation of the Incense Altar, highlighting its significance in the eyes of God. This altar, made of fine gold, serves as a symbol of purification—a process through which we are refined and made ready to commune with the Holy Spirit. As we allow God to purify us like fine gold, the impurities are removed, making it easier for the Holy Spirit to work within us.

Scripture underscores the importance of this purification process in our prayer life. In Psalms 141:2, David prays, "May my prayer be set before you like incense," highlighting the desire for our prayers to ascend as a pleasing fragrance to God. When we are purified like refined gold, our prayers become more aligned with God's will, and we can confidently approach the throne of grace, knowing that our requests will be heard.

As believers, we are called to be vessels of honour, sanctified and set apart for God's purposes. Just as the Incense Altar was placed before the ark of the testimony in the Tabernacle, we are positioned before the presence of God, ready to offer our prayers and intercessions. In Revelation 5:8, the prayers of the saints are likened to incense, signifying their acceptance and fragrance before God.

Ultimately, the Incense Altar serves as a reminder of the transformative power of God's grace in our lives. Through the refining process, we are made vessels fit for the Master's use, empowered by the Holy Spirit to offer up prayers that ascend as a sweet aroma to God. As we embrace this journey of purification and prayer, our joy is made complete, knowing that we stand in the presence of a loving and merciful God who hears and answers our prayers according to His will.

As I reflected on the concept of heaven and its open entrance, I can't help but feel a sense of awe and wonder. It's like standing at the threshold of something so magnificent and breathtaking, yet just beyond my grasp. The Old Testament, with all its rich imagery and symbolism, offers us a glimpse into the beauty and majesty of heaven. It's like catching a fleeting glimpse of a distant paradise, a place where our souls long to dwell.

But more than just a distant dream, heaven serves as a beacon of hope and promise for believers like me. It's the ultimate destination, the final reward for a life lived in faith and obedience to God. And while the Holy Spirit provides us with glimpses of heaven's glory, it's through Jesus Christ that we truly understand its significance. He is the bridge that connects us to the promise of heaven, the one who opens the door and invites us in.

As I ponder on heaven's open entrance, I'm reminded of the importance of preparing my heart and soul for that glorious day. It's not just about waiting passively for heaven to come to me; it's about actively living out my faith and walking in obedience to God's Word. It's about cultivating a deep and intimate relationship with Him, knowing that heaven is not just a destination but a state of being in His presence.

So, as I journey through life, I do so with the knowledge that heaven's open entrance awaits me. It's a source of comfort and reassurance, knowing that no matter what challenges or trials I may face, heaven is my ultimate home. I have seen a bit of it and nothing can really describe it. And as I continue to live out my faith here on earth, I do so with the hope and expectation of one day entering through those gates again and experiencing the fullness of God's glory for all eternity.

POWER *of* WORSHIP

As I reflect on the profound significance of worship, I am reminded of its transformative power in my life that took me to the place we call heaven, where the presence of God lives and dwells.

Worship is not just a ritual or a routine; it is a sacred journey that leads us into the very presence of God. It is through worship that I was able to encounter the divine and experience His overwhelming love and grace.

Worship serves as my invitation to stand before the majestic God, to lay my heart bare before Him and offer Him the reverence and adoration He deserves. It is a reminder that I was created for the purpose of worship, designed to glorify and honour God with every fiber of my being. And as I engage in worship, I find fulfillment and purpose in fulfilling this divine calling.

Looking around me, I see the universal longing for worship ingrained in the hearts of humanity. It transcends cultural and religious boundaries, manifesting in various forms across the globe. Whether it's through music, prayer, or ritual (dancing, raising our hands clapping), every human soul yearns to connect with something greater than themselves. And in worship, we find that connection, that deep resonance with the divine.

But beyond its cultural and religious manifestations, worship holds a profound spiritual significance. It has the power to move the heart of God, to draw us closer to Him and experience His presence in a tangible way. Through worship, I was able to enter into the glory of God, to bask in His love and goodness, and to find peace and fulfillment in His presence. Since then, I became addicted to worship as I know the power it holds.

As I continue on my journey of worship, I am always reminded of its central place in my relationship with God. It is not just an act of devotion, but a lifeline that sustains and nourishes my soul. And so, I commit myself to worshiping God with all that I am, knowing that in His presence, I find true joy, peace, and fulfillment.

Reflecting on my journey from Hinduism to Christianity, I am struck by the profound impact that worship has had on my spiritual life. Growing up in a Hindu household, worship was ingrained in my daily routine. It was a lifestyle, a habit that shaped my relationship with the divine.

When I embraced Christianity, I carried this innate inclination towards worship with me, directing it towards the God of heaven and earth.

Worship, for me, is not merely a religious obligation but a deep and personal expression of my faith. It is a sacred moment where I connect with God on a profound level, pouring out my heart in reverence and adoration. Through worship, I find solace, strength, and joy in the presence of God.

One of the most profound realizations I've had is the power of corporate worship within the body of Christ. Coming together with fellow believers to lift our voices in praise and worship creates a powerful synergy that transcends individual experiences. There is a unique anointing and presence of God that manifests when His people unite in worship, and I have witnessed firsthand the transformative power it holds.

I have experienced the tangible impact of worship in drawing me closer to the throne of God. It is in those moments of worship that I feel His presence in a tangible way, and I am reminded of His love, grace, and faithfulness.

As I continue to walk this path of faith, I am committed to making worship a central aspect of my relationship with God, knowing that it is through worship that I find true intimacy and communion with Him.

Drawing upon the power of praise and worship has been instrumental in my life. In those early months after I became a Christian, the presence of God manifested in every services through worship, drawing crowds eager to experience His glory. One Sunday morning stands out vividly in my memory, a moment when I felt prompted to step out of my comfort zone and ask the people of God to worship, the atmosphere shifted, and I felt the tangible presence of God filling the room.

The voices of the congregation blended into one harmonious chorus, and I found myself lost in the worship, unwilling to break the flow of God's Spirit moving among us. What started as a hesitant step of faith turned into a powerful encounter with the living God.

Witnessing the transformative impact of that worship session was awe-inspiring. The glory of God descended, and many in the congregation were touched by His power, falling under His presence to their knees weeping. The experience ignited a passion within me to continue ministering, leading me to countries and places I never could imagine that experienced the same thing.

It has never stopped, when the Holy Spirit comes in a room and the atmosphere becomes thick, something incredible happens. The miracle power of God manifests with signs and wonders, healing and deliverance.

Through obedience and a willingness to step out in faith, God can use even our most unlikely talents to usher in His presence and touch lives in ways we never imagined. As I continue to serve Him, I am committed to embracing the power of worship as a catalyst for revival and transformation, both locally and across the nations.

When I learned to worship from the depths of my heart, it transformed not only my spiritual life but also my entire being. There's something profound that happens when we pour out our adoration to the Father, acknowledging His supremacy and declaring His worth. It's not just a ritual or a duty; it's a sacred exchange where our love meets His presence in a divine encounter.

In those moments of heartfelt worship, my spirit resonated with a sense of belonging and connection to God. It was as if my spirit man found its true home, enveloped in the embrace of His love and grace. There's a power that emanates from genuine worship, creating an atmosphere ripe for God's presence to manifest in tangible ways.

As we lift our voices and hearts in worship, we join in the heavenly chorus described in Revelation, where every creature in heaven and on earth declares the worthiness of the Lamb of God. It's a profound realization that our worship is not just a solitary act but a part of something much greater—an eternal symphony of praise resounding throughout the heavens.

Through worship, we align ourselves with the heartbeat of heaven, where God's glory reigns supreme. It's a humbling experience to stand in awe of His majesty and to offer our heartfelt adoration as an offering of love. In those moments, we are reminded of our purpose—to glorify God and enjoy Him forever.

I carry with me the transformative power of worship. It's not just a Sunday routine or a set of songs; it's a lifestyle—an expression of love and devotion to the One who gave His all for me. And in every moment of worship, I find myself drawn closer to His presence, experiencing His love and grace in ways that words cannot fully express.

As I reflect on the truth revealed in the Bible, I'm reminded that worship is woven into the very fabric of our existence. From the majestic beauty of creation to the intricate details of our lives, everything points to the greatness of our God. Scriptures like Psalms 48:9-10, Psalms 19:1, Psalms 96:1, Psalms 100:1, and Psalms 148:1-13 emphasize the call to worship the Lord with reverence and awe.

It's fascinating to think that our worship here on earth is just a glimpse of what awaits us in heaven. The thought of standing before the Almighty God, surrounded by the heavenly host, fills me with anticipation and wonder. It's a foretaste of the eternal worship described in Hebrews 12:22-24—a glorious union with the saints and angels in the presence of God.

What's beautiful about worship is its accessibility. It's not confined to a specific time or place but can be experienced anywhere, whether alone in quiet solitude or in the midst of a bustling congregation. No matter our differences or circumstances, we all have the privilege to enter into the sacred space of worship.

At its core, worship is about intimacy—a heart-to-heart connection with the Creator of the universe. It's about acknowledging who God is and who we are in Him. As we focus our attention on His majesty and power, we're reminded of His faithfulness, goodness, and unfailing love. Worship becomes a journey of rediscovering the depths of our relationship with God and surrendering ourselves to His sovereign will.

I'm committed to making worship a central part of my existence. Whether through song, prayer, or simply meditating on His Word, I long to cultivate a heart of worship that honors God in every aspect of my life. And as I do, I trust that my worship will not only bring delight to the Father's heart but also draw me closer to His presence, where true joy and fulfillment are found.

One truth resonates loud and clear: we were created to worship God. Verses like Psalms 48:9-10, Psalms 19:1, Psalms 96:1, Psalms 100:1, and Psalms 148:1-13 paint a vivid picture of our innate desire to honor and glorify our Creator. It's ingrained in the very essence of our being.

The concept of worship isn't confined to a specific time or place; it's a continual posture of the heart. Whether I find myself alone in quiet reflection or gathered with fellow believers in corporate worship, the opportunity to express adoration to God is ever-present. Regardless of our diverse backgrounds and experiences, we all have the ability to enter into the sacred space of worship.

At its core, worship is about acknowledging the worthiness of God. When I stand before the Almighty, I recognize His value not only to me personally but to the entire world. It's a humbling realization that propels me to ascribe honor and reverence to His name.

True worship goes beyond outward expressions or religious rituals; it begins with an inward posture of the heart. It's about reminding myself of who I am in God and meditating on His greatness. As I focus on His majesty and power, I'm drawn into a deeper communion with Him, forging a heart-to-heart connection.

Jesus Himself emphasized the essence of true worship when He spoke to the Samaritan woman at the well. He made it clear that worship isn't confined to physical locations or religious traditions but is a matter of the spirit. It's about approaching God with sincerity and authenticity, worshiping Him in spirit and truth (John 4:24).

Throughout Scripture, we find countless examples of genuine worship—from the angels in heaven who continually praise God to the heartfelt expressions of individuals like Abel, David, and the elders in Revelation. Their worship wasn't bound by formalities or rituals but flowed from a sincere heart overflowing with love and reverence for God.

I'm reminded that worship isn't just a part of my Christian life; it's the essence of it. It's a sacred invitation to commune with the Creator of the universe, to declare His worthiness, and to experience the transformative power of His presence. And as I embrace this truth, I find myself drawn ever closer to the heart of God, where true worship finds its fullest expression.

In the pages of Revelation, I discover a profound truth: even the elders and angels in the heavenly realm conduct themselves before God in worship, bowing down and proclaiming, "Holy is the Lord God Almighty, Who was, Who is, and Who is to come." It's a powerful image that speaks to the essence of worship—declaring the greatness of God.

Through the Psalms, I'm struck by the heartfelt expressions of worship found within its verses. Whether it's meditating on God's character or offering thanksgiving for His deeds, the focus is always on who God is. Worship isn't confined to church gatherings; it's a lifestyle woven into the fabric of everyday life.

Standing before Almighty God, I'm reminded of His unfailing love that surrounds me. Each morning, I purposefully acknowledge His love, knowing that it's His love that ushers His presence over His people. In His love, I find safety and assurance, trusting that He desires the best for His children and will never abandon us.

My faith is strengthened as I contemplate God's divine love. It's a love that assures victory and fills me with unshakeable hope. In worship, I declare God as the creator of all things, knowing that His power knows no bounds and He is fully capable of meeting every need. As His presence fills the atmosphere, I'm enveloped in the reality of His love, releasing a tangible power that touches everyone present.

In worship, I'm reminded that the character of God is boundless, and my expressions of worship—whether through thoughts, words, or actions—are just a glimpse of His infinite greatness.

Cultivating a heart of worship transforms every aspect of life, bringing about profound change and ushering in the presence of God in every circumstance. And, as I continue to deepen my worship, I'm certain that everything around me will be touched and transformed by His love.

Every part of my being is engaged—the mind, the will, and the heart. Growing up in a religion that worshipped millions of gods, I understood the intellectual need that drove such beliefs. Yet, deep within, I longed for a connection with God that went beyond mere intellectual satisfaction. I yearned to worship the one true God who resonated with my heart.

Training my mind to worship God as the only One requires a shift in perspective. It means letting go of the notion that God needs assistance or companionship and embracing the truth that He is self-sufficient and worthy of all worship.

As I redirect my intellectual desires towards the singular God who moves at the sound of my worship, my faith deepens and my connection with Him grows stronger.

Surrendering my will to God is perhaps the greatest challenge of all. It requires humility and obedience to align my desires with His. Yet, as I yield myself to the Creator, my will becomes His, and I find a newfound sense of purpose and direction in His presence. It's a transformation that empowers me to live according to His perfect will.

Then, there's the heart—the seat of our emotions and capacity to love. Through worship, God's love permeates every corner of my heart, replacing hatred with compassion and bitterness with forgiveness. As I immerse myself in worship, I begin to see the world through the eyes of the Holy Spirit, and my heart beats in rhythm with God's heartbeat for humanity.

The impact of worship is undeniable, especially in the lives of new believers who have experienced the transformative power of God's love. Their passion for evangelism and their desire to share the love of God with others is a testament to the profound change that worship brings. It's a language of love that transcends words, drawing others into the embrace of God's unfailing love.

In the realm of worship, there's often a gap between what we know as true worship and what we practice. Some are unaware of the depth of worship, while others resist changing their mindset about how God should be worshipped.

It becomes evident that true worship is not about performance but about honoring God with sincerity and reverence.

Becoming a true worshipper requires steadfastness and dedication. It's like wearing a wedding ring—not just on the wedding day, but every day thereafter, until death parts us. Worship becomes a way of romancing God, fostering intimacy with Him that goes beyond mere rituals and routines.

When I stand before the crowd, I recognize two forms of worship: the vertical and the horizontal. Vertical worship is the direct connection between me and God, where my heart reaches out to His throne. It's a powerful expression of my faith, capable of shifting atmospheres and ushering in the presence of God.

On the other hand, horizontal worship involves the collective praise of God's greatness among believers. Together, we sing songs that exalt His name and encourage one another in faith. It's a beautiful symphony of voices lifting up the name of Jesus.

Vertical worship, however, holds a special place in my heart. It's the intimate dialogue between me and my Creator, where I pour out my love and adoration for Him. It's like singing love songs to God Himself, declaring His majesty and goodness.

As I reflect on the worship described in Revelation, I'm reminded of the heavenly chorus that never ceases to exalt

God's name. It's a glimpse into the eternal worship that awaits us in heaven—a worship untainted by pride or animosity, but pure and rich in its expression of love for God.

I've come to understand the power of the will. Surrendering my will to God's and allowing His Spirit to lead me opens the door to true worship. It's a sacrificial act that brings about a profound connection with God and unleashes His supernatural power in my life.

Ultimately, worship is the key that unlocks the door to the Holy of Holies, where the glory of God dwells. As I draw closer to Him in worship, He draws closer to me, fulfilling His promise to never leave nor forsake me.

In surrendering my will and embracing true worship, I find myself ushered into the presence of the Almighty, where His glory shines brightly, illuminating every corner of my life.

I *saw* HEAVEN

Step into a realm where time stands still, and the ordinary fades into insignificance. This is the world I found myself in when I caught a glimpse of heaven—an experience that forever changed my perspective on life and eternity.

It's not every day that one gets to peer into the celestial realm, to witness the beauty and majesty that await beyond mortal understanding. Yet, here I am, eager to share the profound sights and sensations that unfolded before me.

But before I delve into the details, let me paint a picture for you. Imagine yourself surrounded by an ethereal glow, enveloped in a peace so profound it seems to emanate from the very fabric of the universe. In this sacred space, worries and cares melt away, replaced by a sense of awe and reverence for the divine.

It was in this hallowed atmosphere that I stood, my heart brimming with anticipation as I gazed upward. What I saw surpassed all expectations—a scene of unparalleled beauty and wonder, where every sight and sound spoke of the glory of God.

It was in this hallowed atmosphere that I found myself, standing on the threshold of eternity, with my heart pounding in anticipation of what lay beyond. As I gazed upward, my senses were overwhelmed by the sheer magnificence of the scene before me. It was as though I had been transported to a realm of boundless beauty and wonder, where every sight and sound spoke of the glory of God.

In the moments that followed, I was swept away on a journey of unimaginable proportions, a journey that would take me to the very door of God's throne room. And as I reflect on that remarkable experience, I am filled with a sense of gratitude and humility, knowing that I have been blessed with a glimpse of the eternal home that awaits all who believe.

It's a journey that will challenge your perceptions, stir your soul, and leave you in awe of the boundless love and grace of our heavenly Father. Welcome to my story of how I saw heaven.

After my miraculous healing at the hands of Jesus, I was consumed by a fervor unlike anything I had ever experienced before. It was as if a fire had been ignited within my soul, driving me to seek out the source of this miraculous power that had transformed my life.

I became a fanatic for Jesus, a zealot on a quest to know Him more deeply and intimately than ever before. I would spend hours each day in prayer and meditation, pouring out my heart to the one who had healed me and saved my soul.

But it wasn't enough for me to simply know about Jesus; I wanted to share His love and grace with the world around me. So I took to the streets, preaching to anyone and everyone who would listen, from the birds in the trees to the fish in the sea. I was determined to make known the name of Jesus to all creation.

One Sunday morning, as I stood at the altar with my fellow believers, we began to sing a hymn that would change my life forever. "All hail the power of Jesus' name," we sang, and as the words echoed through the sanctuary, I felt something stirring deep within my soul.

Suddenly, I found myself caught up in a vision unlike anything I had ever experienced before. It was as if I had ascended to heaven itself, standing before the throne of God with the person of the Holy Spirit by my side. Together, we crowned Jesus Lord of all, declaring His sovereignty over every aspect of our lives.

In that moment, I realized the incredible privilege we have as believers to have a relationship with the Holy Spirit, the very

Spirit of the Living God. Though we may not be able to see Him with our physical eyes, we can experience His presence in our lives in a very real and tangible way.

He becomes more than just a distant deity; He becomes our constant companion, our closest confidant, and our greatest source of strength and comfort leading us closer to Jesus and what He did for us on the cross. He fills every part of our being until we are utterly consumed by His love and presence, addicted to the sweet communion we share with Him.

Have you ever wondered if it's possible to be addicted to someone? To crave their presence, to long for their touch, to find solace in their embrace? I used to ponder this question often, especially as I reflected on my own journey with the Holy Spirit.

And, Yes, I believe it's entirely possible to be addicted to a person, especially when that person fills a void within you, when they bring joy to your heart and happiness to your soul. And if a mere mortal can have such a profound impact on our lives, how much more can the spirit of the Living God?

I've experienced it firsthand. The Holy Spirit isn't just a distant deity Jesus spoke about, but He is here on this earth to lead, guide and instruct us. He's a constant companion, a faithful friend, and a loving person. He's there with me every moment of every day, ready to comfort me in times of need, to guide me in times of uncertainty, and to rejoice with me in times of joy.

Spending time with God isn't just about going through the motions of religious rituals; it's about cultivating a deep and intimate relationship with the very essence of your soul. It's about opening your heart to His presence, allowing Him to fill every empty space within you with His love and grace.

Back to what happened on that Sunday morning at church. It was a Sunday morning, like any other, and I found myself standing among the congregation, singing praises to the King of Kings. As the familiar hymn, "All Hail The Power of Jesus' Name," echoed through the sanctuary, something extraordinary happened.

Suddenly, I felt myself being lifted, not by human hands, but by the unseen power of the Holy Spirit. It was as if He had wrapped His gentle arms around me and carried me away from the earthly realm into the heavenly realm on five occasions.

In an instant, I was transported to a place beyond description. I found myself standing before a massive door, towering high above me, adorned with intricate carvings and radiant with light. It was the entrance to the throne room of God.

As the door swung open before me, I was bathed in a brilliant light that radiated warmth and love. It was unlike anything I had ever experienced on earth, a light so pure and intense that it seemed to penetrate to the very depths of my soul.

And there, standing next to the blinding brilliance of the light, was a figure. It was like a shadow, yet somehow more tangible, more real. I couldn't make out the details of the person's face, but I could sense their presence, their power, their majesty. I knew it was Jesus.

In that moment, I knew without a doubt that I was in the presence of the Almighty God. The One who created the heavens and the earth, the One who holds the universe in His hands, the One who knows the number of hairs on my head and the thoughts in my heart.

It was a moment of awe and wonder, of reverence and fear. But above all, it was a moment of overwhelming love. For in the presence of God, there is no room for fear or doubt, only perfect love that casts out all fear.

As I stood there, bathed in the light of His presence, I felt a peace that surpassed all understanding wash over me. It was as if every worry, every care, every burden was lifted from my shoulders, and I was enveloped in the arms of my Heavenly Father.

And in that sacred moment, I knew that I was exactly where I was meant to be. In the presence of the King of Kings, the Lord of Lords, the Alpha and the Omega. And as I gazed upon His glory, I couldn't help but crown Him Lord of all in my heart and in my life.

As I saw the throne of God, I am enveloped by a holy atmosphere unlike anything I've ever experienced. It's as if the very air around me pulsates with His presence, filling me with a sense of awe and reverence. This holy atmosphere is tangible, almost palpable, and it draws me closer to the throne with each step I take.

I remember the first time I felt this way was during a time of deep prayer and meditation, when I felt compelled to seek God's presence with all my heart at 14 years old.

As I entered into His throne room, I was overcome by a sense of peace and tranquility that I had never known before. It was as if all the cares and worries of the world melted away in the presence of His glory.

The throne of God itself is a sight to behold. It radiates with a brilliance that is both blinding and beautiful, a reflection of His majesty and power. And surrounding the throne are beings of unimaginable splendor - the cherubim and seraphim - whose voices ring out in praise and adoration, filling the heavens with their heavenly song.

But it's not just the sights and sounds that make this atmosphere holy; it's the very essence of God Himself that permeates every corner of the throne room. His holiness is like a consuming fire, purifying and sanctifying all who enter into His presence. And as I stand before Him, I am acutely aware of my own unworthiness, yet overwhelmed by His boundless love and grace.

In this holy atmosphere, time seems to stand still. It's as if eternity itself unfolds before me, and I am caught up in the wonder of His glory. Here, in the presence of the Almighty, all earthly concerns fade away, and I am left with nothing but a sense of wonder and awe at the beauty of His holiness.

As I reflect on this sacred space, I am reminded of the words of Isaiah, who beheld the throne of God and cried out, "Holy, holy, holy is the Lord of hosts; the whole earth is full of His glory!" (Isaiah 6:3). And like Isaiah, I am humbled by the privilege of standing in the presence of such holiness, and filled with a desire to worship and adore Him for all eternity.

As I stood in the presence of God, my eyes were opened to the breathtaking beauty of the heavenly realm. It was like nothing I had ever seen before, a place of indescribable wonder and majesty.

Everywhere I looked, there was evidence of the glory of God. The walls of the throne room seemed to shimmer and glisten like pure gold, yet softer, more radiant. It was as if the very essence of gold had been transformed into liquid light, flowing and dancing before my eyes.

And the floor beneath my feet was a mosaic of precious stones, each one more dazzling than the last. Opals, diamonds, sapphires, rubies – they all shimmered and sparkled in the light of God's presence, casting reflections that looked like the sun rays piecing through the clouds.

But it was what lay beyond, at the very back of the throne room, that truly took my breath away. There, bathed in the brilliance of the Almighty, was a display of pure radiance. It was as if the sun itself had descended from the heavens and cast its rays upon the earth, illuminating everything in its path with a warmth and intensity that was both awe-inspiring and humbling.

As I gazed upon this magnificent sight, I felt a sense of peace and wonder wash over me. It was as if every worry, every care, every fear was swept away in the presence of such beauty and majesty. And in that moment, I knew that I was standing on holy ground, in the presence of the One who created all things.

It was a moment I would never forget, a glimpse into the glory of God that would stay with me for the rest of my days. And as I stood there, surrounded by the splendor of the heavenly realm, I couldn't help but praise Him with all my heart, for He alone is worthy of all honor and glory and praise. The more I worshipped the Lord, the more I felt I was being drawn into His presence. The atmosphere felt so thick it could but cut with a knife.

As I stood at the threshold of that celestial doorway, bathed in the radiance of divine light, I was overcome by a wave of emotions unlike anything I had ever experienced before, except when I was fourteen years old. It was as if every insecurity, every doubt, every fear was magnified a thousandfold in the presence of such holiness.

In that moment, I felt small and insignificant, like a piece of discarded gum stuck to the sole of someone's shoe. I was acutely aware of my flaws and shortcomings, of every mistake I had ever made, every sin I had ever committed. I felt unworthy, undeserving of even being in the presence of such majesty.

And yet, despite my feelings of inadequacy, there was a voice – soft yet unmistakable – that spoke to me from the depths of my soul. "This is where you belong," He said, with a tenderness that brought tears to my eyes.

But I couldn't accept it. I couldn't believe that I belonged in a place so holy, so perfect. I felt like an imposter, like I was somehow trespassing on sacred ground. "I don't belong here," I protested, my voice barely a whisper in the vastness of that celestial chamber.

But the voice persisted, gentle yet persistent. "You are loved," it said. "You are cherished. You are worthy." And as those words washed over me, something inside of me began to shift. It was as if a light had been ignited in the darkness of my soul, dispelling the shadows of doubt and fear.

In that moment, I realized that my worthiness was not determined by my past mistakes or my present shortcomings. It was not contingent on my own merit or achievements. Rather, it was a gift – freely given, unconditionally bestowed – by the One who created me, who knew me intimately and loved me deeply.

And as I stood there, bathed in the light of that truth, I felt a sense of peace and acceptance wash over me. I may have felt like garbage, but in the eyes of my Creator, I was precious, I was valued, I was beloved. And that realization changed everything.

As I stood before the door, trembling like a beggar in the presence of royalty, I couldn't shake the feeling of unworthiness that clung to me like a heavy cloak. What right did I have to stand before such majesty, to enter into the inner chambers of the King?

But despite my doubts and fears, the King beckoned me forward with a gesture, a feeling of kindness and grace. "Come," He said, His voice like music to my ears.

With trembling steps, I crossed the threshold and entered the room, unsure of what awaited me. And then it happened – something miraculous, something divine.

It was as if a fire was ignited within me, a flame that burned with an intensity I had never known before. Suddenly, my lips were aflame with words, my mouth opening wider than I could have ever imagined. And as I spoke, it was as if a great hand reached down and pulled something from deep within me, something weighty yet light as a feather.

In that moment, I felt a sense of liberation, of freedom, of release. It was as if the chains that had bound me for so long were finally broken, and I was free to soar like a bird on the wing.

I couldn't explain it, couldn't understand it, but I knew that something profound had taken place within me. I had been touched by the hand of the King, anointed with the fire of His presence, and I would never be the same again.

As I stood there, bathed in the warmth of that divine encounter, I knew that I had been chosen, called, set apart for a purpose greater than myself. And with that knowledge came a sense of peace, of purpose, of belonging.

I may have entered the room feeling like a beggar, but I left feeling like royalty – embraced by the love of the King, empowered by His spirit, and forever changed by His grace.

As I stood there, overwhelmed by the fire that now burned within me, I felt a surge of joy coursing through my veins. It was as if every cell in my body was alive with excitement, with anticipation, with the sheer wonder of what had just taken place.

Then suddenly, I saw myself back to earth. I fell to the floor with a feeling of joy unspeakable. I felt like I fell into cushions of feather, soft that the ground did not feel like the ground. It felt like was in that vision for an hour, but yet with was only about fifteen minutes.

But even as I reveled in the afterglow of that divine encounter, I couldn't shake the feeling of confusion that lingered in the back of my mind.

Me, an evangelist? The words the pastor prophesied over me as I stood on my feet. "You would be an evangelist and God will take you all over the world." The thought seemed ludicrous, impossible, utterly beyond the realm of possibility.

After all, I had always been the quiet one, the introvert, the one who preferred the solitude of my own thoughts to the company of others. How could someone like me, someone so comfortable in the shadows, ever step into the spotlight of evangelism?

But as I wrestled with my doubts and fears, a voice broke through the fog of uncertainty – the voice of my friend Joseph Jaggan, the one who had stood by my side through thick and thin, through joy and sorrow, through triumph and tribulation.

"Let's put this prophecy to the test," he said, his eyes shining with excitement. "Let's go out into the streets, into the neighborhoods, into the very heart of our village, and share the good news of Jesus Christ with everyone we meet." I never stopped sharing the gospel from that day.

As I conclude my recount of the awe-inspiring experience of glimpsing heaven, I can't help but feel overwhelmed by the profound impact it has had on me. It's not every day that one gets to catch a glimpse of the celestial realm, but for me, it was a moment that I will carry with me for the rest of my days.

The vivid imagery and overwhelming sense of peace and joy that enveloped me as I beheld the beauty of heaven is something I struggle to put into words. It was as if time stood still, and all worries and cares melted away in the presence of such divine majesty.

What struck me the most was the sense of belonging and serenity that washed over me. In that moment, I knew without a doubt that heaven is real, and it is a place of indescribable beauty and perfection. It was a glimpse into eternity, a reminder of the hope that awaits all who believe in the promise of salvation.

But beyond the breathtaking landscapes and celestial wonders, what truly left an impression on me was the overwhelming sense of love that permeated every corner of heaven. It was a love so pure and unconditional, unlike anything I had ever experienced on earth. It filled me with a sense of awe and gratitude, knowing that I am cherished and deeply loved by the Creator of the universe.

As I reflect on my encounter with heaven, I am reminded of the fleeting nature of life on earth and the eternal promise of life beyond. It has renewed my faith and deepened my longing for the day when I will be reunited with loved ones in the presence of God.

Though I may never fully comprehend the mysteries of heaven, I am grateful for the glimpse I was given. It serves as a beacon of hope and a reminder of the ultimate destination that awaits all who place their trust in God. And until that day comes, I will carry the memory of heaven in my heart, allowing it to inspire and guide me on my journey of faith.

THE *throne room* EXPEREINCE

Entering into the throne room of God is an experience unlike any other. As I step through the threshold, I am immediately enveloped in a sense of awe and reverence. The atmosphere crackles with an electric energy, pulsating with the very presence of the Almighty. It's as if every molecule in the air is charged with His glory, and I can feel His presence like a tangible force surrounding me.

The first thing that captures my attention is the throne itself. It sits at the center of the room, towering above everything else, radiant with a brilliance that is both dazzling and comforting. It's a sight that takes my breath away, reminding me of the majesty and sovereignty of the One who sits upon it. And as I gaze upon the throne, I am filled with a sense of peace and assurance, knowing that I am in the presence of the King of kings and Lord of lords.

Surrounding the throne are beings of incomparable beauty and power - the cherubim and seraphim. Their presence is overwhelming, and their voices resound through the room like thunder, filling the air with the sweet melody of worship and adoration. It's a symphony of praise unlike anything I've ever heard, and it moves me to the very core of my being.

But it's not just the sights and sounds that make this experience so profound; it's the overwhelming sense of His glory that permeates every aspect of the room. His glory is like a tangible presence, filling the room with a warmth and light that is both comforting and awe-inspiring. It's a presence that I can feel deep within my soul, stirring me to worship and adoration.

As I stand in the presence of God's glory, I am overcome with a sense of humility and reverence. In His presence, I am acutely aware of my own shortcomings and failures, yet I am also filled with a sense of His love and grace. It's a love that knows no bounds, a grace that covers all sin, and it draws me ever closer to Him.

In this throne room experience, time seems to stand still. It's as if the cares and worries of the world fade away, and all that matters is the presence of the Almighty. Here, in His presence, I find peace and rest for my soul, and I am filled with a sense of purpose and destiny.

As I reflect on this throne room experience, I am reminded of the words of the psalmist:

"One thing I have desired of the Lord, that will I seek: that I may dwell in the house of the Lord all the days of my life, to behold the beauty of the Lord, and to inquire in His temple" (Psalm 27:4).

And like the psalmist, I am filled with a longing to dwell in His presence forever, beholding His glory and experiencing His love in all its fullness.

As I step into the sanctuary, I am immediately aware of the divine presence that permeates the air. It's as if I've entered into a sacred space where heaven meets earth, and the atmosphere is charged with anticipation. This is the throne room of God, where His glory dwells in abundance.

To create the throne room atmosphere, I start by preparing my heart. I quiet my mind and set aside distractions, focusing solely on the presence of God. As I enter into a posture of worship, I feel the weight of His glory descending upon me, filling every corner of the room with His majesty.

Worship is the key that unlocks the door to the throne room. I lift my voice in adoration, singing praises to the King of kings. With each word, I feel the atmosphere shifting, as the angels join in the heavenly chorus, declaring the holiness of God.

As I continue to worship, I sense the presence of God drawing near. His glory surrounds me like a tangible cloak, enveloping me in His love and mercy. In this sacred moment, I am reminded of His faithfulness and goodness, and I am overcome with gratitude.

The throne room atmosphere is characterized by reverence and awe. I bow before the throne of God, acknowledging His sovereignty and power. In His presence, I am humbled, recognizing my own insignificance in comparison to His greatness.

In the throne room, there is a sense of peace and rest. Here, I find refuge from the cares of the world, as I cast all my burdens upon the Lord. In His presence, I am strengthened and renewed, ready to face whatever challenges may come my way.

As I linger in the throne room, I am filled with a sense of purpose and destiny. Here, I am reminded of God's calling on my life, and I am empowered to walk in obedience to His will. In His presence, I find clarity and direction, knowing that He is leading me every step of the way.

The throne room atmosphere is not limited to a physical location—it can be experienced wherever we are. Whether in the quiet of my prayer closet or in the midst of a crowded sanctuary, I can enter into the presence of God and encounter His glory.

As I cultivate the throne room atmosphere in my life, I am transformed from glory to glory. In His presence, I am made more like Him, reflecting His love and grace to the world around me. And as I carry His presence with me wherever I go, I become a carrier of His glory, bringing light and hope to a dark and broken world.

When I think about the power of atmospheres, it's like realizing how every setting influences our thoughts and emotions. Whether it's a cozy coffee shop or a bustling bar, the atmosphere shapes our experiences in profound ways. And when it comes to encountering the glory of God, I've learned that creating the right atmosphere is crucial.

Romancing God feels like standing close to a warm fire on a chilly evening. The love that fills my heart in His presence is worth every effort I put into drawing near to Him. Just like how the heat intensifies the closer you stand to a fire, drawing near to God ignites a deeper passion within me.

Just like how the atmosphere changes before a storm, there's a spiritual energy that precedes the manifestation of God's glory. As believers, we have a responsibility to cultivate an atmosphere where His presence can manifest powerfully. Whether it's through prayer, worship, or intentional fellowship, we have the power to create an environment where miracles can happen.

We're born into a kingdom where the air is thick with the presence of glory. It's an atmosphere so rich that every interaction is infused with positivity. It straightens out life's twists and turns, soothes our pain and sorrow, and brings healing to our souls.

But the enemy knows the power of this atmosphere too well. He's trained his demons to throw up obstacles, hindering individuals and churches from tapping into this divine realm. Yet, I've come to realize that we possess the willpower to break through these barriers and pave the way for God's glory to shine forth. It takes strength of our 'will' to carve out a space where God's presence can thrive.

Once we grasp the art of crafting the right atmosphere, we're primed for God's glory to burst forth. It's about surrendering our willpower to the Holy Spirit and making the necessary sacrifices to create an environment conducive to God's presence. It's akin to stepping into the holy of holies, taking intentional steps toward divine encounter.

With the atmosphere set, we're poised for Majesty to reveal Himself. We can cultivate an atmosphere of celebration, of deep emotions, of reverent silence, or of eager expectation.

Transitioning from the crowd, we enter the outer courts, where communal worship uplifts us. Then, individually, we move into the Holy Place, reflecting on our lives and drawing nearer to God. Emotions may surge as we contemplate God's love and our salvation. We're reminded of the power of the cross, propelling us toward the throne of God, the Holy of Holies.

Even a glimpse of His presence is enough to leave an indelible mark on our souls, confirming that God is indeed alive. And when the right atmosphere is cultivated, it opens the door wide for the presence of God to envelop us.

When I think about the holiness of God, I can't help but feel a sense of awe and reverence wash over me. It's like standing in the presence of something so pure and powerful that it takes your breath away. I remember the first time I truly encountered the holiness of God; it was a moment that changed my life forever.

In that moment, I was acutely aware of my own sinfulness and unworthiness in the presence of His holiness. It was a humbling experience, one that left me trembling with both fear and adoration.

The holiness of God is not something to be taken lightly; it is a consuming fire that burns away everything impure and unholy in its path. It's like standing too close to the sun; its brightness is blinding, yet its warmth is comforting. And just as the sun's light reveals every imperfection, so too does the holiness of God expose the darkness within us.

But despite the overwhelming sense of awe and reverence that accompanies the holiness of God, there is also a deep sense of love and grace. For in His holiness, God reveals Himself as the perfect and loving Father who longs to draw us near to Him. It's a paradoxical truth; His holiness demands perfection, yet His love covers a multitude of sins.

As I meditate on the holiness of God, I am reminded of the words of Isaiah: "Holy, holy, holy is the Lord of hosts; the whole earth is full of His glory" (Isaiah 6:3). These words echo through the ages, proclaiming the majesty and splendor of the One who sits upon the throne. And as I join my voice with the heavenly chorus, I am filled with a sense of wonder and awe at the holiness of God.

In the presence of His holiness, I am compelled to bow down in worship and adoration, for He alone is worthy of all praise and honour. And as I surrender myself to Him, I am transformed by His holiness, purified and made whole. It's a journey that continues each day, as I strive to walk in His ways and reflect His holiness to the world around me.

Ultimately, the holiness of God is not something to be feared but embraced. For in His holiness, we find redemption and restoration, forgiveness and grace. It's a reminder that despite our flaws and failures, God's holiness is greater still, and it is His holiness that sets us free and brings us into His presence forever.

In that moment, as I stood there surrounded by a voice echoed through the room, piercing through the silence. It was the voice of the Lord, and He said to me, "I am holy." His words reverberated within me, shaking me to the core.

I stood there in my brokenness, I was overwhelmed by the truth of God's holiness. It was a holiness that was pure and untainted, a holiness that demanded nothing less than perfection. And yet, it was also a holiness that offered forgiveness and redemption.

It was a humbling experience, one that reminded me of the incredible love and mercy of God.

As I reflected on that encounter, I realized that God's declaration, "I am holy," was not just a statement of His character, but a call to holiness for His people. It was a reminder that as His children, we are called to reflect His holiness in our own lives, to strive for purity and righteousness in all that we do.

And so, I made a commitment to walk in holiness, to live my life in a way that honoured God and brought glory to His name. It was a journey that I knew would not be easy, but I trusted in the power of God's Spirit to guide me and empower me every step of the way.

In the end, I understood that God's holiness was not something to be feared but embraced. It was a standard of righteousness that He had set for His people, a standard that He had provided the means to attain through His Son, Jesus Christ. And as I surrendered myself to His will, I found peace and joy in knowing that I was walking in the light of His holiness.

So, I pour out my soul in worship, as if tomorrow would never come. Every fiber of my magnified the Lord, rejoicing in His saving grace. The more I worshipped, the more my spirit yearned for His presence. It was like a spiritual addiction, drawing me closer to something indescribably wonderful.

Living in the presence of God ceased to be a rare occurrence; it became my daily reality. It was an experience beyond compare, surpassing anything this world could offer. As I basked in His presence, I realized the unparalleled joy and fulfillment it brought.

The words from 1 Kings echoed in my mind, reminding me of the awe-inspiring moment when the glory of the Lord filled the temple, rendering the priests unable to stand. It was a testament to the overwhelming power and majesty of our God, a power that I had the privilege of experiencing firsthand through worship and repentance.

> *"And it came to pass, when the priests come out of the Holy Place, that the clouds fill the House of the Lord, so that the priests could not stand to minister because of the clouds. For the glory of the Lord had filled the House of the Lord".* 1 Kings 8: 10-11

As I stood in the presence of God, His glory manifested all around me, overwhelming me with its power. It was so intense that I couldn't stand; I was brought to my knees by the sheer magnitude of His presence. It was a moment I'll never forget, a moment where I realized that God's glory wasn't confined to a distant place or time – it was here and can be obtained 24/7.

As I began to learn how to cultivate the presence of God in my life, something shifted in the atmosphere around me. The same power that descended upon the priests in ancient times was now tangible in my own living room, in my church, and everywhere I went. The glory of the Lord wasn't just a distant concept; it was a reality I could feel and experience firsthand.

In the midst of this divine encounter, I felt the Holy Spirit working within me, drawing me closer to Himself. It was as if an unseen force propelled me forward, and I found myself falling to my face in worship. All I could utter was the profound truth of the blood of Jesus – that His sacrifice was for the salvation of souls. For what seemed like an eternity, I repeated this truth, feeling the weight of His presence pressing upon me.

As I worshipped, I felt a heaviness of peace descend upon me, rendering me unable to stand. Yet, I continued to press into the presence of God, allowing His Spirit to move within me.

It was as if I was being baptized afresh in the Holy Spirit, my soul melting like wax before the flames of His glory. In that moment, the Holy Spirit performed a deep work within me, renewing and transforming me from the inside out.

As the glory of God filled me, I sensed a tangible change within me. It was as if my very being was infused, signifying the presence of God within me. Yet, as I sought to contain this anointing, the Holy Spirit gently reminded me that His presence couldn't be trapped or contained – it needed to be continually cultivated and maintained.

I soon realized that maintaining the anointing meant cultivating a lifestyle of intimacy with the Holy Spirit, continually seeking His presence and surrendering myself to

His will. Each time I entered into His presence, I had to approach with expectancy and a willingness to die to self, allowing Him to work in and through me.

In the wake of this encounter, my passion for souls was reignited with a newfound fervour. The glory of God had stirred something deep within me, propelling me forward with a renewed drive to see the lost saved. It was a divine commissioning, a call to partner with God in His redemptive work on earth.

When life feels like a storm and heaven seems distant, I've found that worship is the key to unlocking the door to God's presence. Building a strong relationship with the Lord takes time and effort, but the secret place of the Most High is accessible to all of us, regardless of our circumstances.

During moments of despair or exhaustion, I often find solace in the midst of chaos. Sometimes, I'd purposefully immerse myself in the rush hour crowd on the subway, using the hustle and bustle of city life to remind myself of the work that lies ahead. In the faces of strangers, I see glimpses of the divine, reminding me that God is present even in the most ordinary moments.

Entering into God's presence is like stepping into another realm, where His glory dwells and His mark is upon us. It's not a place we visit casually, but when we do, it transforms us in ways we can't imagine. Yet, many struggle to navigate this sacred space, often letting their flesh dictate their actions. But for those who dare to venture in, it's a realm where faith flourishes, fears dissipate, and the true essence of holiness and majesty is revealed.

For me, one of the most valuable lessons came in the form of preparation. Before I could encounter the King, I need to purify my heart, mind, and spirit, making room for His presence to dwell. And when He comes, there is the importance of maintaining that level of readiness, ensuring that I could enter His presence.

I am filled with awe and gratitude for the experiences I've had and the lessons I've learned. Stepping into the presence of God is not just a momentary encounter; it's a transformative journey that shapes who we are and how we live our lives.

In the Throne room, I've experienced the overwhelming power of God's glory, the profound depths of His love, and the unmatched beauty of His holiness. It's a place where time seems to stand still, where worries fade away, and where I am enveloped in the embrace of my Heavenly Father.

Each visit to the Throne room has left an indelible mark on my soul, reminding me of my true identity as a beloved child of God. In His presence, I am renewed, restored, and empowered to live a life of purpose and passion.

But the Throne room is not just a destination; it's a calling—a beckoning to draw near to God, to seek His face, and to dwell in His presence continually. It's a reminder that

He is always with me, guiding me, strengthening me, and filling me with His Spirit.

As I conclude this chapter of my journey, I carry with me the precious memories of my time in the Throne room. And with each step forward, I walk in the confidence that no matter where life may take me, I can always return to the Throne room—the place where heaven touches earth and where I am forever changed.

GLORY REVEALED

Experiencing the incredible glory of God and feeling His presence is truly like no other sensation. It's a profound warmth that fills me with pleasure, happiness, and an overwhelming sense of joy. In those moments, time seems to lose all meaning, as if an hour could pass in the blink of an eye. It's a sacred space where every emotion is heightened, and I'm reminded of the purpose and significance of my faith.

In the midst of God's glory, I find a deep understanding of who I am in Him and the profound impact of His love in my life. It's as if a veil has been lifted, revealing the depth of His grace and the incredible sacrifice Jesus made for me. The presence of the Holy Spirit becomes palpable, guiding me and filling me with a sense of peace and purpose.

Being in God's presence is like being wrapped in a comforting blanket, soothing my body, soul, and spirit. It's a sanctuary where I find solace and strength, knowing that His love surrounds me always. In those moments, I feel truly blessed and grateful for the joy and peace that only He can provide.

As I reflect on the glory of God, it's like trying to capture the essence of a breathtaking sunset or the majesty of a mountain peak. It's beyond words, yet I'll do my best to paint a picture of what it means to me. When I think of God's glory, I imagine radiant light enveloping everything around me, filling the air with a sense of awe and wonder.

In the Bible, the glory of God is often described in terms of light and brilliance. In Exodus 24:17, it says, "To the Israelites, the glory of the Lord looked like a consuming fire on top of the mountain." Can you imagine being in the presence of such divine radiance? It's like standing before a blazing fire, feeling its warmth and power, yet being completely captivated by its beauty.

But the glory of God isn't just about light; it's also about His presence. In Exodus 33:18-19, Moses asks to see God's glory, and the Lord responds by saying, "I will cause all my goodness to pass in front of you." The goodness of God is like a sweet fragrance that fills the air, comforting and reassuring those who draw near to Him.

And then there's the taste of God's glory. In Psalm 34:8, it says, "Taste and see that the Lord is good; blessed is the one who takes refuge in him." When we experience the goodness of God, it's like savouring the most delicious meal, feeling nourished and satisfied in every way.

But perhaps the most profound aspect of God's glory is how it transforms us. In 2 Corinthians 3:18, it says, "And we all, who with unveiled faces contemplate the Lord's glory, are being transformed into his image with ever-increasing glory." When we spend time in God's presence, we can't help but be changed. It's like being in the presence of a master artist who is continually shaping and molding us into something beautiful.

So, what does the glory of God look like to me? It's like standing in the midst of a radiant light, feeling the warmth of His presence, savouring the goodness of His love, and being transformed into His likeness. It's an experience that words can't fully capture, but one that leaves me in awe of the greatness and majesty of our God.

As I meditate on Haggai 2:6-9, I'm reminded of the profound words of the Lord Almighty promising to once more shake the heavens and the earth, filling His house with glory. It's a reminder that God's glory is not just a concept but a tangible reality that can shake the very foundations of the earth. Throughout history, God has revealed His glory in extraordinary ways, leaving a mark on those who have witnessed it.

I think back to the Israelites in the wilderness, following a pillar of cloud by day and a pillar of fire by night. Imagine being surrounded by such a visible manifestation of God's glory, guiding and protecting you every step of the way.

Then there's the image of the temple filled with a cloud of glory, a tangible representation of God's presence among His people. It's awe-inspiring to think about how God chose to reveal Himself in such a tangible way.

And then there's Moses, who had the incredible privilege of seeing God's glory firsthand. The experience was so intense that his face radiated with its reflection, a physical manifestation of being in the presence of the Almighty. It's a reminder that encountering God's glory leaves a lasting impression, transforming those who experience it from the inside out.

Even in the vision of Ezekiel, we see the glory of God depicted as a figure surrounded by a brilliant light of rainbow colours. It's a reminder that God's glory is beyond our comprehension, encompassing all the beauty and majesty of creation.

And let's not forget the shepherds who witnessed the glory of the Lord shining around them at the announcement of Christ's birth. It's a reminder that God's glory is not confined to the pages of history but is still revealed to us today.

Reflecting on God's glory, I'm reminded that it's unlike anything else in this world. While humans may seek power, recognition, and eminence, God's glory is unique in its intrinsic worth and permanence. It's a reminder that true fulfillment and joy come from experiencing the presence of God, basking in His glory, and being transformed by His love.

As I reflect on the words of Isaiah, "My glory I give to no other," I'm reminded of the divine uniqueness of God and His unmatched supremacy. His glory is not just a distant concept but a tangible reality that permeates His very being and creation. God's glory is intimately intertwined with His identity, and there's no separating the two.

The ultimate manifestation of God's glory is found in His Son, Jesus Christ. In the Gospel of John, we're told that Jesus is the Word made flesh, dwelling among us, full of grace and truth.

This profound truth underscores the radiance of God's glory shining through Christ, who is described as the exact representation of God's being. In Jesus, we see the embodiment of divine glory, a beacon of hope and truth in a world shrouded in darkness.

Christ's sinless life serves as a powerful testament to the glory of God. As He walked among humanity, His light pierced through the darkness of sin, offering hope and courage to all who encountered Him. Even in His most vulnerable moments, such as His crucifixion, the mercy and compassion of God were made manifest, offering forgiveness and redemption to all who believe in Him.

The miraculous acts performed by Jesus further reveal the glory of God. From healing the sick to raising the dead, His actions were a testament to His divine nature and the boundless love of the Father.

The transformation of water into wine at Cana of Galilee and the raising of Lazarus from the dead are just a few examples of how Jesus revealed God's glory through His miraculous deeds.

The radiant faces of Moses and Stephen, who beheld the glory of God, serve as a poignant reminder of the transformative power of divine encounter.

Just as Moses' face shone after being in God's presence, we too can reflect the Lord's glory in our lives as we draw closer to Him.

The mount of transfiguration, where Peter, James, and John witnessed the visible glory of God on Jesus' face, serves as a testament to the transformative nature of divine encounters.

As believers, we are called to reflect the Lord's glory in our lives, undergoing a process of transformation into His likeness. This transformation is not static but ongoing, with ever-increasing glory bestowed upon us by the Holy Spirit.

As I ponder Paul's words about the glory of God in the New Testament, I'm struck by the contrast he draws between the fading glory of the Old Testament and the enduring glory of the New. It's a reminder that God's glory is not static but ever-lasting, and it's made manifest to us through the Holy Spirit.

The Holy Spirit, who dwells in glory, has chosen to make His home within us, bringing with Him the fullness of God's glory. It's a humbling thought to consider that the same glory that filled the temple in the Old Testament now resides within us.

Paul's teachings emphasize that having the Holy Spirit dwelling within us means that we carry a measure of God's glory wherever we go. Yet, our perception of this glory is limited, like looking through a darkened glass. It's as if we're catching glimpses of God's glory, but we can't fully comprehend its magnitude or beauty. Despite this limitation, we're called to reflect the Lord's glory in our lives, becoming more like Him with each passing day.

In 2 Corinthians 3:18, Paul highlights the transformative power of God's glory at work within us. As we behold the glory of the Lord, we are gradually transformed into His likeness, with our lives radiating His glory more and more each day. It's a process of growth and renewal, fueled by the presence of the Holy Spirit within us.

Peter also speaks of the Spirit of glory resting upon those who are insulted for the sake of Christ. This reminds us that the glory of God is not just a personal experience but something that shines forth from us, even in the face of adversity. When we face persecution or ridicule because of our faith, the Spirit of glory sustains us, giving us strength and courage to endure.

I'm reminded of the privilege and responsibility we have as bearers of God's glory. It's a profound truth that the same Spirit who raised Christ from the dead now lives within us, empowering us to live lives that reflect His glory to the world around us.

One striking example is the cloud and pillar of fire that guided the Israelites through the wilderness for 40 years. Imagine the awe and wonder they must have felt as they witnessed this supernatural display of God's glory, leading them day and night. Yet, despite experiencing His glory in such a profound way, the Israelites often fell into disobedience and rebellion against God, demonstrating that His presence alone did not guarantee holiness.

In the Old Testament, we encounter numerous instances where God's glory is visibly manifested, such as when the cloud covered the Tabernacle by day and the pillar of fire illuminated the night sky. These tangible displays served as reminders of God's presence and power among His people.

However, as I ponder these accounts, I realize that they pale in comparison to the measure of the Holy Spirit poured out on believers in the New Testament.

Peter's words in Acts 2:17-21 echo in my mind, affirming that the Holy Spirit is not limited by age, gender, or social status. The promise of the Holy Spirit is for all believers, young and old, male and female.

Through the indwelling presence of the Holy Spirit, we have access to a dimension of God's glory that surpasses anything experienced in the Old Testament. It's a glorious reality that we can tap into as we prepare ourselves for spiritual warfare and seek intimacy with the Lord.

As I contemplate the significance of the Holy Spirit's presence in my life, I'm filled with a sense of awe and gratitude. The Holy Spirit is not merely a distant observer but a faithful companion and guide, leading me into deeper fellowship with God and empowering me for service. With the Holy Spirit dwelling within me, the possibilities are endless, and I am encouraged to press forward in my journey of faith, knowing that I am not alone.

When God's love fills the atmosphere, it's like opening the floodgates for His glory to flood in. The more love there is, the more His glory manifests itself. It's like a gentle breeze that begins to swirl around us, permeating every corner of our being. And the Holy Spirit, our faithful helper, is right there with us, guiding us as we press in, worship, and build ourselves up in anticipation of encountering His glory.

I've experienced moments where the presence of God becomes tangible, almost like you could reach out and touch the air. It's in those moments that the atmosphere becomes so thick with His glory that you can almost feel it weighing down on you.

People around me have fallen to their knees or even collapsed under the weight of His presence. It's a humbling and awe-inspiring experience, one that leaves me in awe of His power and majesty.

During these encounters with God's glory, hearts are softened, and souls are convicted of sin. Tears flow freely as people are overcome with emotion, and the Holy Spirit moves in miraculous ways. It's in these moments that healing takes place—mentally, emotionally, physically, and spiritually. The fruits of the Spirit come alive, and joy fills the air, making us feel stronger and more alive than ever before.

I often marvel at the transformative power of love. When love is the driving force behind our worship and our interactions with one another, amazing things happen. As individuals and as a community, we become vessels for God's glory to flow through, and His presence becomes palpable in our midst. The gifts of the Spirit are unleashed, and lives are forever changed.

Just a glimpse of His glory is enough to sustain us for a lifetime. In those moments of encounter, we catch a glimpse of eternity, and it changes us in ways we can't even begin to fathom. The value of our lives is forever altered as we become immersed in the glory of God, forever marked by His love and presence.

The first time I truly delved into the concept of "glory" was when I stumbled upon the story of Moses. His encounters with God, veiled in the brilliance of His glory, left me in awe and wonder. I embarked on writing this book, I uncovered a note tucked away in my files, dated back to 1989, detailing six Hebrew words for glory. Each word offered a unique perspective:

Hader - representing "beauty" and "excellence."

Tohar - embodying "purity" and "brightness."

Sebhi - signifying respect for a prominent figure.

Adderith - suggesting something "broad," "big," and "unbounded."

Hodh - capturing the grandeur and majesty of God.

Kabod - conveying notions of "weightiness," "authority," and "courageousness."

Inspired by these ancient meanings, "glory" encompasses a multitude of concepts: whatever brings honour, praise, and adoration; divine happiness; the pinnacle of excellence or prosperity; and splendor or brilliance that captivates the senses.

As I reflected on these definitions, I realized that the notion of glory extends far beyond mere radiance or grandeur. It encapsulates the essence of everything that is praiseworthy, admirable, and divine. It's the culmination of all that is good and righteous in the world, emanating from the very heart of God Himself.

I've come to see it as a multifaceted gem, reflecting different facets of God's character and nature. It's His beauty shining forth in creation, His purity illuminating the darkest corners of our souls, His authority reigning supreme over all things. It's the weight of His presence, the richness of His love, and the courage He instills in His people to rise above adversity.

Ultimately, glory is not just a word or a concept—it's an invitation to behold the majesty of God in all His splendor and to bask in the radiance of His love. It's a call to recognize and honour the divine attributes that define His character and to live our lives in pursuit of His glory.

And as I continue on this journey, I'm filled with a deep sense of reverence and gratitude for the privilege of experiencing and proclaiming the glory of God in all its forms.

The glory of God is eternal and unchanging. It's His very essence, radiating from His majestic presence. As 1 Corinthians 9:16 reminds us, our greatest boast should be in preaching the gospel and proclaiming the transformative power of God's glory in our lives.

God isn't just adorned with glory; He is glory, comprising its very essence.

God's glory is unlike anything we can comprehend. It permeates His being, defining His existence and radiating power, majesty, and authority. Imagine the atmosphere in which God dwells—the very air He breathes is infused with

His glory, and His presence illuminates everything around Him. His glory is not just a part of Him; it's His life source, the energy that sustains all of creation.

Even when Jesus walked the earth in human form, He was enveloped in the glory of God. In the Gospel of John, we read about the miraculous signs Jesus performed in Cana of Galilee, revealing His glory to His disciples and inspiring belief in Him among the people. His divine glory was evident to those who witnessed His works and encountered His presence.

The apostle John offers us a glimpse into the glory of Christ in John 1:14, where he describes Jesus as the Word made flesh, dwelling among us, full of grace and truth. Jesus, the express image of God's person, radiated the brightness of His glory, upholding all things by the word of His power.

Even before His earthly ministry, Jesus shared in the glory of the Father, as described in John 17:5, 22, and 24. He longed for His followers to share in that glory, to behold His majesty and splendor as He had experienced it before the world began.

The concept of God's glory can sometimes feel abstract, but one way to understand it is as a "weight," signifying its immense worth and significance. From a biblical standpoint, glory represents the splendor of God Himself, the radiance of His presence. It's like the light that emanates from His very being, revealing His majesty and worthiness.

When we speak of God's glory, we're acknowledging His full deity and majesty, which is present in every place and manifests His power in tangible ways. It's a weighty presence, akin to power or influence, that can be felt and experienced.

Thinking about the weight of God's presence reminds me of my first experience at the gym. I had friends who had been lifting heavy weights for years, but I had never given much thought to weightlifting or its purpose.

One day, I decided to join my friends at the gym. They were starting with bench pressing 90 pounds, just a warm-up weight for them. Confidently, I grabbed the weight bar and attempted to lift it as they did. However, my lack of experience in the weight room quickly became apparent when the bar almost came crashing down on me. It was a humbling lesson in the importance of knowing our own limits and building strength gradually.

Reflecting on that experience, I realized there was a parallel to be drawn between physical strength training and spiritual growth. Just as we strengthen our muscles through exercise, spending time in God's presence exercises our spiritual muscles and enables us to lift the weight of His glory. The more we invest in spiritual exercise, the stronger and more confident we become in navigating the challenges of life.

Sometimes, we may underestimate our spiritual strength until we encounter others who are not as strong. Our spiritual growth can inspire and uplift those around us. It's not about being better than others, but rather about recognizing the unique strengths and gifts that each person brings to the table.

Consistency is key in both physical and spiritual exercise. Just as a dedicated gym-goer commits to daily workouts, a committed Christian prioritizes regular time in God's presence. It's not about relying on others to lead us or waiting for the next spiritual high; it's about cultivating our own personal connection with God and allowing His glory to transform us from the inside out.

The secret to experiencing the fullness of God's glory lies in dwelling in His presence. Like a warm blanket enveloping us, His peace and joy overflow in our hearts, filling us with a sense of contentment and security. In that sacred space, the Holy Spirit moves freely, bringing healing, restoration, and miracles. It's a place where salvation is tangible, and the power of God is evident in every aspect of our lives.

I'm reminded of the longing in my own heart to experience God's glory firsthand. It's like a deep yearning, a thirst that can only be quenched by His presence. I find myself echoing the psalmist's cry, "Show me Your glory," desperate to catch just a glimpse of His majesty.

As this longing grows within me, so does my passion to live a life that honours God. I realize that experiencing His glory requires more than just passive observation—it demands an active pursuit of righteousness and holiness.

This pursuit fills me with a sense of purpose and dedication. I'm willing to do whatever it takes to draw closer to God, to carve out moments in my day where I can seek Him wholeheartedly.

Time becomes irrelevant as I prioritize communion with Him above all else, knowing that in His presence is where I truly belong.

And in this pursuit, I find a newfound freedom and confidence. I trust in God's power to part seas and move mountains in my life, knowing that nothing is too difficult for Him. My faith is bolstered by the knowledge that He can work wonders through ordinary people like me, transforming my weaknesses into strengths and my doubts into unwavering belief.

Ultimately, my desire to see God's glory isn't just about experiencing a momentary spectacle—it's about forging a deeper connection with my Creator. It's about drawing nearer to Him and allowing His glory to illuminate every aspect of my life. And as I continue on this journey, I'm filled with hope and anticipation for the wonders He has yet to reveal.

"DON'T TAKE *your* GLORY AWAY..."

I remember when I felt the weight of God's glory in my life like never before. I felt His peace, His joy, and His strength sustaining me through every trial and triumph.

But then, something shifted. Life got busy, distractions crept in, and I found myself gradually drifting away from that place of closeness with God. Without even realizing it, I began to take His glory for granted, assuming it would always be there whenever I needed it.

It wasn't until I started to feel the emptiness and uncertainty creeping back into my life that I realized the gravity of my mistake. I had allowed the busyness of life to overshadow the importance of nurturing my relationship with God. I had taken

His glory for granted, assuming it would always be there without putting in the effort to seek it out.

As I reflected on this realization, I was reminded of the words of King David in Psalm 51:11, where he pleads with God, "Do not cast me from your presence or take your Holy Spirit from me." It was a sobering reminder that God's glory is not something to be trifled with or treated lightly.

I knew I needed to make a change, to recommit myself to seeking God's presence and honouring His glory in my life. So I made a conscious effort to carve out time each day for prayer, worship, and Scripture reading. I sought out opportunities to serve others and share the love of Christ with those around me.

And slowly but surely, I began to feel God's presence returning to my life in a powerful way. His peace once again filled my heart, His joy overflowed in my soul, and His strength sustained me through every trial. I realized that His glory was not something to be taken lightly—it was a precious gift to be cherished and nurtured.

So now, whenever I feel myself starting to drift away from God's presence, I remember the lesson I learned: "Don't take your glory away." I make a conscious effort to prioritize my relationship with Him above all else, knowing that His presence is the greatest treasure I could ever hope to possess. And as I continue to seek Him with all my heart, I know that His glory will never be far from me.

Seeking the glory of God has been a burning desire within me ever since I discovered its potential. I realized that sin is what separates us from experiencing the fullness of God's glory, as Romans 3:23 makes clear. Yet, as I committed my life to serving Him, I began to understand that living in alignment with His will could bring forth His glory in remarkable ways. It became evident to me that without His presence, His glory remains veiled, but when His presence manifests, extraordinary feats become possible.

Whenever I step into a ministry moment or lead worship, my singular focus is to press into the spiritual realm until something supernatural occurs. It feels like traversing into another dimension, where the supernatural presence of God awaits. And once I grasp hold of that presence, akin to Jacob, I refuse to let go.

Reflecting on Jacob's wrestling encounter in Genesis 32:24-28, I draw inspiration. Jacob tenaciously wrestled with the divine until he received a blessing. He refused to release his grip until he obtained a divine encounter, and as a result, his life was forever changed.

Similarly, I've learned that in my pursuit of God's glory, I must be relentless, unwavering in my determination to experience His presence.

There have been moments in my spiritual journey where I've sensed the tangible weight of God's glory, moments where His presence felt almost palpable. It's during these times that

I've witnessed miracles unfold, chains of bondage shattered, and lives transformed.

These encounters serve as a reminder of the power and majesty of our God, fueling my hunger for more of His glory.

Just as Jacob's name was changed to Israel after his wrestling match, signifying his transformation, I've experienced my own metamorphosis in the presence of God's glory. It's in those sacred moments of divine encounter that I've been changed, strengthened, and empowered to fulfill my purpose.

So, I continue to press on, longing for more of His glory, refusing to settle for anything less than a profound encounter with the living God. For in His presence, I find fulfillment, purpose, and the assurance that I am walking in alignment with His divine will.

Developing stamina in my spiritual journey has been a crucial lesson I've learned. I realized that merely going through the motions won't lead me into God's presence; it's a heart fully engaged in worship that draws me nearer to Him.

It took time for me to understand the importance of persistence and discerning the spiritual atmosphere around me. But as I cultivated a desire to encounter God, I committed to staying focused until I experienced a breakthrough.

Entering into the presence of God often feels like stepping into another realm, where His tangible presence envelops me.

Sometimes it's as if a warm blanket wraps around me, or I feel a tingling sensation as if the hairs on my body are standing up. Other times, it's like my limbs are melting away, and a profound sense of peace washes over me, suspending time and space. In these moments, it's just me and God, and the rest of the world fades into the background.

Encountering God's glory stirs my emotions, evoking tears of joy or conviction. It's a transformative experience that leads me into the secret place of the Most High, if only for a fleeting moment.

In this sacred space, I feel liberated, free from guilt, pain, confusion, and worry. It's as if I'm floating in a cloud of God's glory, experiencing a taste of heaven on earth. This momentary encounter fills every emptiness within me, leaving me whole and complete.

It's a place I believe we were destined to inhabit—a divine connection between Creator and creation, where nothing and no one can steal away the joy and peace found in His presence. In these moments, brokenness is repaired, hurts are healed, and emptiness is replaced with abundance.

No amount of worldly wealth can purchase entry into this sacred space; it's a heart-to-heart connection with God Himself.

As I reflect on the promises of God, I'm reminded that His faithfulness is unwavering. He has sealed me with His Spirit, providing a glimpse of His glory that leaves me yearning for more. And in these moments, I find assurance that His promises are true and that His glory is revealed through me.

The departure of the glory of God from the temple in Ezekiel's vision served as a sobering reminder of what happens when His presence is forsaken. I shuddered at the thought of the glory of God leaving my life, and it spurred me to realign my focus and prevent myself from falling further away.

In the New Testament, the glory of God finds its ultimate expression in Jesus Christ. John's words in John 1:14 echoed through my mind, reminding me that the Word became flesh and dwelt among us, revealing His glory to humanity. It was a message of redemption and restoration, a promise that His glory could once again shine brightly in my life.

Though the road ahead may be challenging, I knew that His presence was worth every sacrifice and struggle. With each step forward, I moved closer to experiencing the fullness of His glory, a treasure beyond compare.

The Holy Spirit, residing within us, serves as a beacon of God's glory. He is a vital part of the Godhead, intimately acquainted with the power and majesty of God's presence. Despite His holiness, He chose to dwell among sinful humanity, offering us a pathway to experience the glory of God firsthand. He stands as the key to unlock the door to God's glory, ready to work with anyone willing to bring glory to Christ.

Imagining the sorrow of the Israelites as they witnessed the departure of God's glory is heart-wrenching. It was their source of comfort, hope, faith, security, and support—a tangible reminder of God's presence among them. In my own life, I felt like a ship anchored in place, unable to move forward.

The Holy Spirit gently nudged me to lift the anchor weighing me down, but it proved too heavy for me to handle alone. I needed the Holy Spirit, my Helper, to become my close companion once more.

Ezekiel's vision of the glory of God filling the temple stirred my soul. It reminded me of God's promise to dwell among His people, bringing joy and restoration. Scripture after scripture echoed this promise, renewing my hope and driving me to seek the face of the Lord with renewed fervour.

I remembered the covenant I made with God years ago, and His faithfulness overwhelmed me. In His presence, I feel at home, guided by the Holy Spirit into the depths of His glory. It is a reunion with my Creator that I had sorely miss.

As I reflect on the journey of safeguarding the glory of God in my life, I'm reminded of the invaluable treasure it is. I've come to realize that I never want to feel empty again, to lose something so priceless and precious. The Holy Spirit, who ushers in the presence of God, has taught me what I need to do to remain in that sacred space.

It's not just about experiencing the glory of God once; it's about cherishing it, guarding it, and allowing it to transform every aspect of my life. I've learned that I must continually seek God's presence, allowing the Holy Spirit to guide me and keep me close to Him. It's a daily commitment, a conscious choice to prioritize the presence of God above all else.

I've also learned the importance of humility and dependence on God. I can't take His glory for granted or rely on my own strength to sustain it. Instead, I must surrender to Him completely, trusting Him to keep me in His presence and protect His glory within me.

In the end, I understand that the glory of God is not just for my benefit alone. It's meant to be shared with others, to shine brightly in a dark world and lead others to experience the fullness of God's love and presence.

CONCLUSION

As I come to the conclusion of sharing my encounter with God's throne room in this book, I'm reminded of the profound journey it has been to revisit those sacred moments. Over 40 years have passed since that transformative experience, yet the memories remain as vivid and powerful as ever. It's as if time stood still in that divine presence, leaving an indelible mark on my soul.

Recalling the surge of power, the warmth, and the overwhelming sense of God's presence that enveloped me upon entering the throne room, I am filled with awe once again. Standing before those grand doors, with the Holy Spirit as my guide, I was ushered into a realm of beauty and splendor beyond comprehension.

Though words fall short in capturing the full extent of what I witnessed, I have endeavoured to offer a glimpse of that divine encounter within the pages of this book. From insights into creating an atmosphere conducive to encountering God, to the profound significance of worship, to a brief description of the majestic throne room itself, I have sought to share the essence of my experience.

But even as I lay down my pen, I know that this journey is just the beginning for each reader who embarks on it. For in these pages lies not just a recounting of my personal encounter, but an invitation to explore the depths of God's presence and the glory of His kingdom for yourself.

May this book serve as a catalyst for transformation in your life, as you open your heart to the possibility of encountering God in new and profound ways. May you be inspired to seek His presence with renewed fervour, and may His glory shine brightly in every area of your life.

As I bid farewell, I do so with the hope that " My Story Of Heaven" will not just be a book you read, but an experience that leaves an indelible mark on your soul—a reminder of the boundless love and glory of our Creator.